# TRADITIONAL WINDSOR CHAIR MAKING

## WITH JIM RENDI

Basic, step-by-step
instructions
for building
a comb back
Windsor chair

D1558593

77 Lower Valley Road, Atglen, PA 19310

Text written with and photography by Douglas Congdon-Martin

**DEDICATION**
To Andrea, for all her help and support.

Published by Schiffer Publishing, Ltd.
77 Lower Valley Road
Atglen, PA 19310
Please write for a free catalog.
This book may be purchased from the publisher.
Please include $2.95 postage.
Try your bookstore first.

We are interested in hearing from authors
with book ideas on related subjects.

Printed in the United States of America
ISBN: 0-88740-503-7

# Contents

# Introduction

The early part of the 18th century witnessed the arrival of the Windsor chair in the colonies from England. It did not take long for American craftsmen to begin manufacturing their own chairs. This most likely began in Philadelphia; early advertisements in Boston newspapers promoted the "Phila. Windsor Chair." As the demand for the chairs increased so did the number of chairmakers involved in making them. Before long the designation of "Philadelphia" was dropped, and each region and each chairmaker began to make his own innovations and impact on the designs of the chairs.

The comb-back Windsor represents the height of the hand-crafted era. At the same time it is a manifestation of the soundness and the graceful beauty of the design. The name "comb-back" refers to the back of the chair, which resembles a comb. Its simple, delicate appearance belies a construction that is strong and flexible. The construction techniques are the hallmark of the hand-made Windsor. The two most important, integral aspects of this are the tapered joinery, and the hand-split lumber. Michael Dunbar, one of America's leading authorities on Windsors, says that without these two features the chair is worthless. The past two hundred years have given us time-tested proof of the chair's endurance in use. A visit to Independence Hall or the Winterthur Museum will give you a renewed appreciation for the work of our predecessors.

Everything about the Windsor chair was purposefully designed as a system, both internally and externally. By its nature, wood is in a state of constant motion. No matter what finish it has, it is absorbing and giving off moisture. As it does so, the wood expands and contracts. (For further understanding of the argoscopic properties of wood see J. Alexander's *Make a Chair Out of Green Wood.*) The result of this motion is the tendency toward loose joints in the chair.

To counteract this tendency, the Windsor chair is designed with tapered joinery. Every time someone sits in a Windsor chair, his weight has the effect of tightening the seat. This contrasts with round tenon joinery or the post and rung construction of a chair like the ladder back. In both of these chairs the shrinking of the wood leads to a natural looseness and the slight twisting motion of the sitter can create quite a problem. A comparison of the two types of joinery makes clear the genius of the Windsor design.

The comb-back Windsor in this book represents an adaptation of the first fifty years of the style's development. We will go back in time to the height of the hand-crafted era, just before the Industrial Revolution. It was the time of the signing of the Declaration of Independence and the American revolution, when the concept of "interchangeable" parts was being introduced by the Elis brothers.

The earlier comb-back Windsor differed from ours in a few details. The Philadelphia chair usually had a "D" shaped seat, while ours will have a seat that is oval. The leg turnings of the earlier chair may have ended in a blunt arrow design. Also called a "goat's foot," the leg ended in an egg or oval section with a blunt or flat spot to allow it to sit level on the floor. The tapered baluster leg in this book is an economical and progressive adaptation, saving labor and time while giving the leg a streamlined look and appeal. Finally we will use a steam-bent arm, rather than the earlier sawn-arm design. The handholds will be shaped in a scroll pattern resembling a musical notation.

To make the comb-back Windsor chair in this book we will use the same type of tools that the early craftsmen did: the gutter adz, scorp, chairmaker's bits (spoon bits), draw-knives and spokeshaves. It will recapture the era of the latter eighteenth century, when a one-man shop could specialize in the making of Windsor chairs.

I work in a 1792 carriage shed, but any garage or basement will do as well. A few of the tools will have to be constructed or customized, but you should have no trouble doing this.

The Windsor chair has enjoyed a steady popularity since its introduction. In part it is because it brings together quality, endurance, and simplicity. It reflects the nature of its maker in an almost intimate way. It is a specialized craft that is, at the same time, both refined and common.

I teach workshops for people who have come under the enchantment of the Windsor chair. Those who come to me usually have another profession, but are seeking something more for their lives. They are attracted to Windsor chair making, because it involves creativity. Working with wood seems a natural thing to do, and while they are forming their chairs they have a sense of freedom and exhilaration. I hope you enjoy the project in this book in the same way, and that you come to love the Windsor chair form as much as I do.

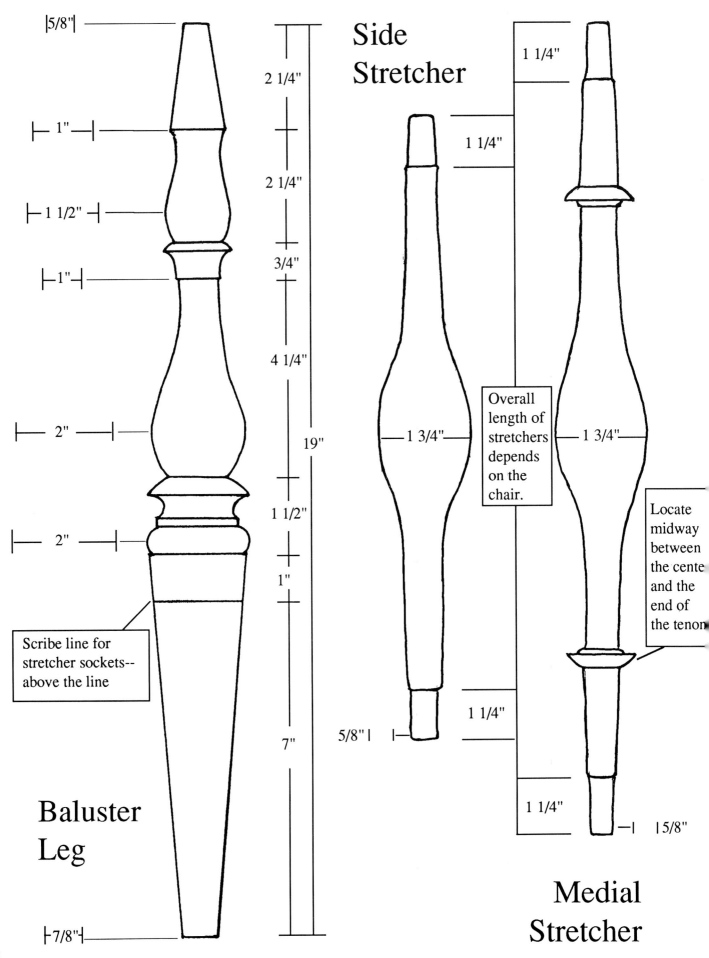

5/8"

2 1/4"

1"

2 1/4"

1 1/2"

3/4"

1"

4 1/4"

2"

19"

2"

1 1/2"

1"

**Scribe line for stretcher sockets-- above the line**

7"

**Baluster Leg**

7/8"

6

**Side Stretcher**

1 1/4"

1 1/4"

1 3/4"

**Overall length of stretchers depends on the chair.**

5/8"

1 1/4"

1 1/4"

1 1/4"

1 3/4"

**Locate midway between the center and the end of the tenon**

1 1/4"

5/8"

**Medial Stretcher**

# Arm Scroll
## Actual Size

The arm scroll is a decorative addition to the ends of the arm piece. The overall dimensions of the arm piece are:

    Length: 44"
    Thickness: 3/4"
    Width: 5/8"

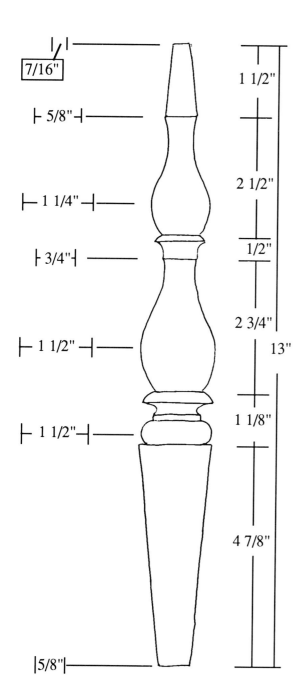

7/16"

1 1/2"

5/8"

2 1/2"

1 1/4"

1/2"

3/4"

2 3/4"

1 1/2"

13"

1 1/8"

1 1/2"

4 7/8"

5/8"

## Arm Post

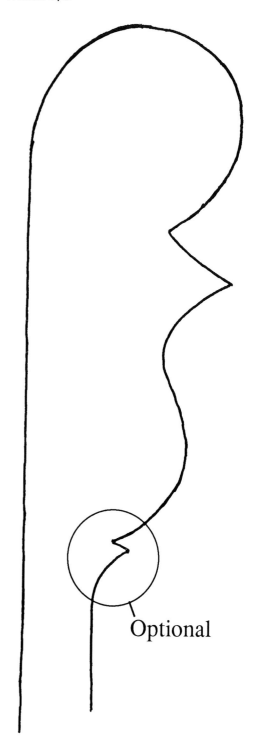

Optional

# The Seat

9/16" sockets spaced approximately 2 5/8" apart. A divider seperated each hole evenly.

Small gouge groove around the spindle area. An 1/8" gouge can be used.

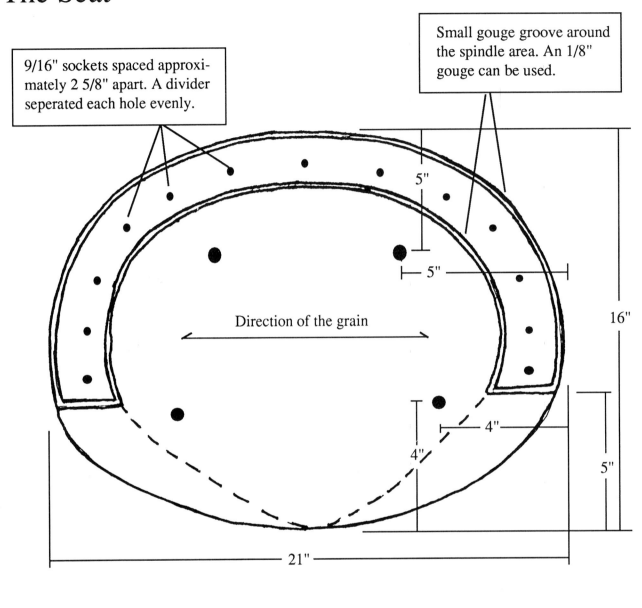

Direction of the grain

5"

5"

16"

4"

4"

5"

21"

The depth of the excavation in the seat varies from 1/4" to 1".

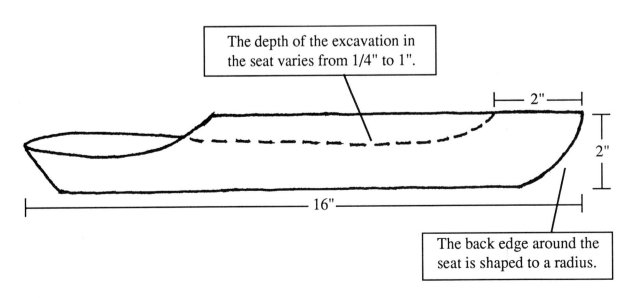

2"

2"

16"

The back edge around the seat is shaped to a radius.

# Bending Jigs

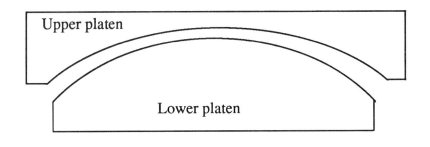

Upper platen

Lower platen

## For the comb

A method to bend the comb is to use solid members known as the platen system (upper and lower). For our chair a slight curve of 5" should work, though you may choose to tighten or loosen the curve. Usually the side chair version of the comb back Windsor, or the fan back, has a more pronounced curve than the arm chair.

The platen form has two parts. The difference between them is that the lower form has a tighter or smaller radius. This difference allows the forms to tighten more evenly around the piece to be bent.

Both parts can be made up from scrap wood. This form needs only a few clamps.

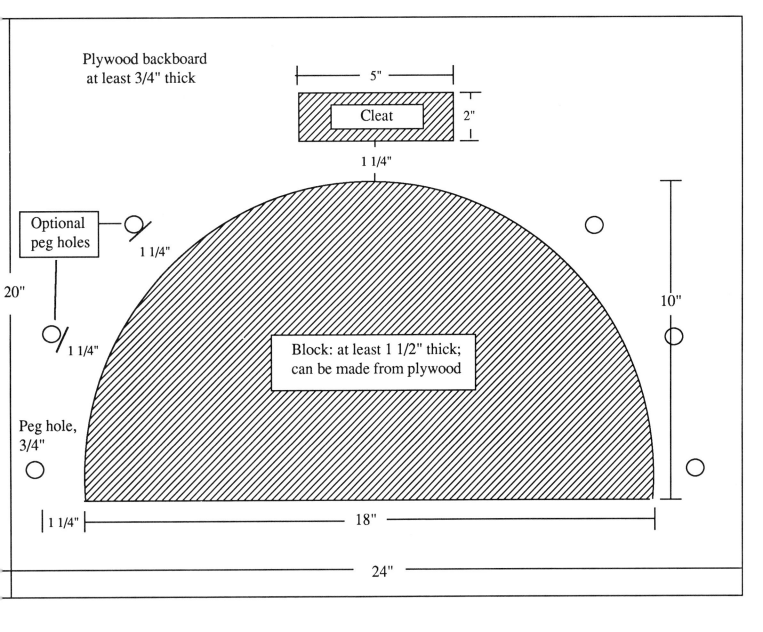

Plywood backboard
at least 3/4" thick

5"

Cleat

2"

1 1/4"

Optional
peg holes

1 1/4"

1 1/4"

20"

10"

Block: at least 1 1/2" thick;
can be made from plywood

Peg hole,
3/4"

1 1/4"

18"

24"

# The Comb

Actual size: from center to one end. Use to create a pattern from cardboard.

Dimensions:   3/4" thickness
             28 1/2" total length
             3" height

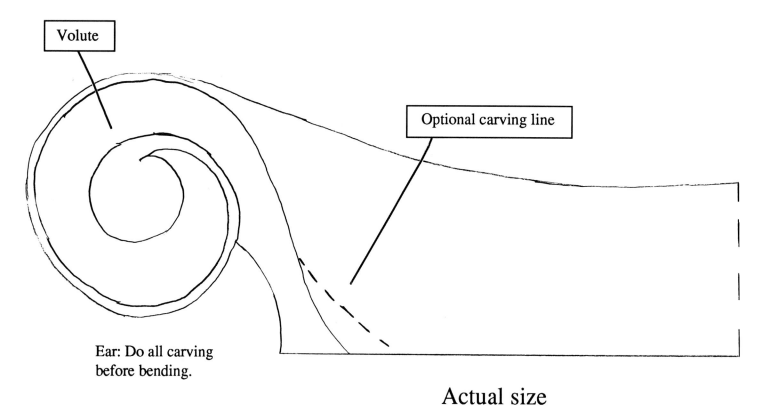

Volute

Optional carving line

Ear: Do all carving
before bending.

## Actual size

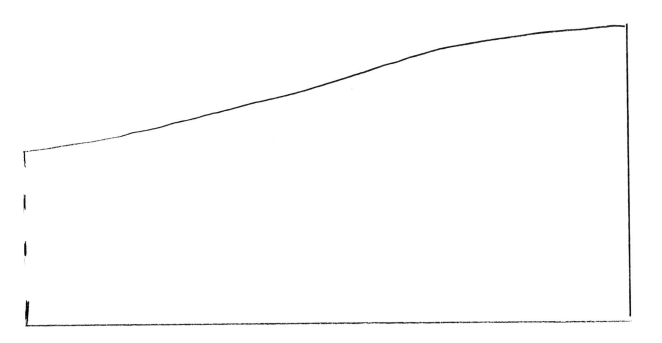

# Splitting the Wood for Legs and Stretchers

Use a close grained wood, like maple or birch for the legs and the stretchers of the undercarriage. In eastern Pennsylvania we use black birch. The wood does not have to be aged, though after splitting you will let it season a few days before turning. The log you buy should be a little longer than five feet to get three 20″ sections. It should be between twelve and sixteen inches in diameter. Smaller and you are working too close to the heartwood. Bigger and you have a log that is too bulky to handle. Not only is log lumber much cheaper than sawn lumber, it is easier to use and better for the chair. To find log lumber, contact the forestry service in your area. They should be able to supply you with the names of local loggers.

When buying wood in log form you usually look closely at the bark to determine the straightness of the grain or the presence of knots. You want the straightest, cleanest wood possible for turning. Unfortunately with birch that is often hard to tell from the outside, so we have to split it to see.

One of the only power tools I use is the chain saw to cut the log to length. Always use the proper safety equipment when using power tools. In this case I have ear protection, safety glasses, and heavy leather gloves.

With the log in the pile like this I cut as far as I can and use a cant hook to turn it.

Measure the log for the legs, marking every twenty inches.

Continue the process until the log is cut in billets. With a log this thick, each section should provide enough wood for the undercarriage of three or four chairs.

This piece already has a natural check, so we start our splitting there.

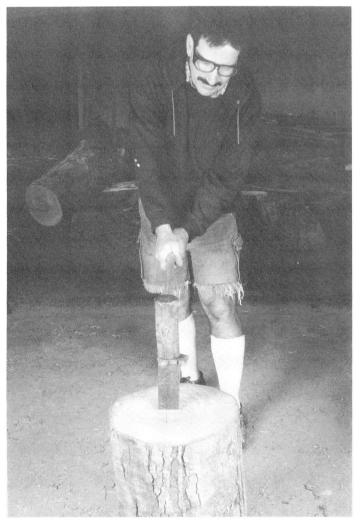

I use a variety of tools for splitting the wood. On the left are froes. They have a triangular blade with a dull edge for splitting rather than slicing. The older ones are cast in a single piece and they have a handle of about 20″. Next are wedges which come in a variety of sizes. Don't use a wedge that has mushroomed at the top from use. There is a chance that it will break off and cause injury. The froe club was turned on the lathe. A broad axe with a wide shape will go through a wide piece of wood. Finally you should have a sledge hammer, the power source. The head is of a softer metal than that used for stone.

Drive in the wedge using the sledge hammer.

Drive a second wedge to divide the half into quarters.

Continue splitting the quarters. Leave the wedges in place until they come loose. With a straight grained wood, like we have, this happens naturally, but sometimes you have to work at it. Split until the log is divided into eighths.

A third wedge creates four quarters. Again, I've followed naturally occurring splits.

Next we split concentrically. Make a mark two inches from the bark.

Make a mark that divides this outside piece in two.

Three pieces can usually be derived from each eighth section of the log. Continue on each wedge of the log. Because splitting is not an exact science, some wedges will yield only two pieces.

Mark in from the first mark another two inches. Unless it has straight grain, the heart wood will not be used, saving a lot of problems.

Split the wedges into the smaller sections marked.

For the final split it is good to use the froe and froe club. The wooden froe club is used against the metal froe to preserve your tool.

The heart wood has knots and wavy grain and needs to be removed. Use the froe to split it off.

The axe is handy for cutting the remaining splinters that hold the sections together.

With a few minutes work, the log becomes 24 usable pieces. I now let them sit for a couple days before rough turning.

# Making a Froe Club

Use a piece of hard wood about 5″ in diameter and 24″ long. Load it into the lathe and use a wide gouge to bring the piece to round shape. The wide gouge will quickly remove the wood. Always use a safety mask when using the lathe.

Use the large gouge to shape the club back to the handle.

Using the parting tool, partition the ring of the handle. Cut in to a diameter of 1″.

Use a smaller gouge to make an astragal on the end of the handle. The handle should be comfortable to hold.

# Turning the Legs

Take a billet and align it in the lathe, eyeballing the approximate center and lightly adjusting the head and tail pins. Turn the piece by hand to make sure it lines up with the center of the lathe. Make any adjustments and tighten it down.

Turn the billet to a round shape using the wide gouge.

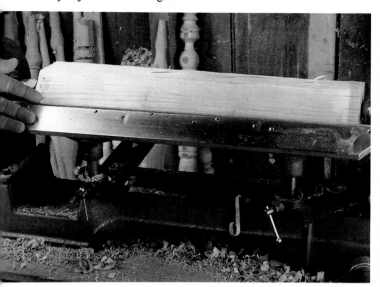

I use a tool rest that is the whole length of the piece I am turning. This means you can go through the whole turning without having to move anything.

Set a caliper to 2″ and with a parting tool cut a depth gauge.

Remove enough wood to bring the whole billet to 2″ diameter.

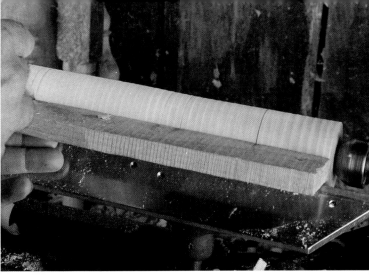

Align your tool rest with the axis of the lathe. Hold the gauge up to the billet and mark the segments. On the gauge, I make a little v-cut on the edge at the mark. This gives a place for my pencil to ride while I mark the spinning billet.

Taper the bottom third of the leg, until it is roughly the size you want it.

Use a parting tool to cut the segment lines to the proper diameters. The first cut I do by eye.

The different segments of the leg are marked on a gauge.

Then use the caliper with the parting tool to get to the exact dimensions. The diameters are given in the measured drawings.

Shape the segments to the diameters set by the parting tool. Always start in the center of a segment and move toward an end.

Reduce the size of the top piece.

Progress.

Shape the bead with the skew. . .

Cut the cove with a lady-finger gouge.

and continue with the wafer here and. . .

Use a pivoting motion to get the shape you want. Move from right to the center, and. . .

further up.

left to the center.

Continue working until you get the nice, deep cove you want.

Continue to give it the overall shape you desire.

Create a half cove under the upper wafer in the same way.

Do the same on the bottom vase.

Shape the upper vase down to the wafer.

Shape the bottom section, then use a scribe to mark the line for the stretcher.

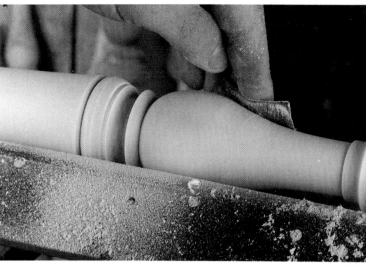

Use a skew to smooth the leg. This takes a light touch and a lot of practice. The skew is a difficult tool to learn, but when you do, it will save a lot of time with sand paper.

Use a fine grade sand paper to smooth the work. For straight areas, simply hold the paper against the turning leg.

For coves and other details, fold the paper in half to create an edge.

Use the skew to make glue lines at the top of the leg, where it will be inserted into the seat. (optional)

Finally take a handful of your shavings and hold it against the spinning piece. This gives a nice, smooth finish.

# Turning the Stretchers

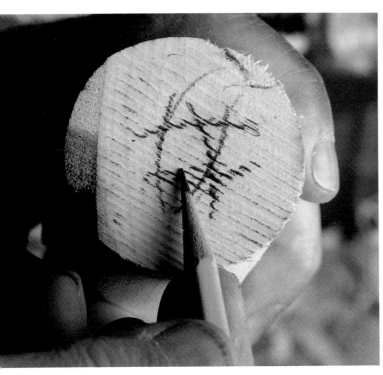

Mount the piece in the lathe. The old-time chairmakers would not have worried about a side like this when making a stretcher. They would simply be sure it was on the bottom of the piece. If it bothers you, however, situate the billet in the lathe so that it is slightly off center. When it's turned, the rough portion will be removed.

I use a drier wood for the stretchers than I do for the legs. I let the wood sit around for a week or so after I rough turn it. The greener wood of the legs will then shrink around the tenons of the stretchers, making a snug fit. The old chairmakers tried to achieve this snugness by having a slight bulbous shape to the ends of the tenons, the duckbill tenon. It was assumed that the naturally occurring shrinkage of wood surrounding the bulbous tenon would make the perfect locked joint that would not give. Unfortunately, even though the joint held together, the shrinkage that occurred on both the tenon and socket allowed the tenon to come loose. The billet for the stretcher should be 1.75″ in diameter. To find the center of the billet, use your finger as a depth gauge and move around the end making marks. The center should become clear.

We begin with the center stretcher. Turn the billet, rounding it down with a large gouge.

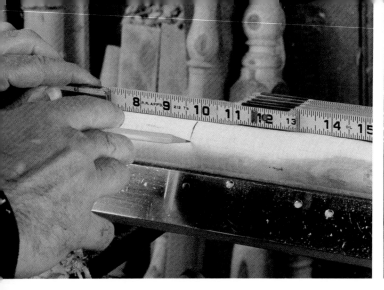

Measure and mark the center of the billet.

The second cut begins ½″ inside of the outer cut.

With the piece turning, scribe to the center and a ring approximately 4″ to either side of it. The rings are approximately ½″ wide.

Shape the center section out to the ring, working from the middle.

The outside rings are a combination of a half-bead and half-cove. Define its size with the parting tool. Cut to about 1″ in diameter.

Work in both directions. While the basic dimensions are established by measure, the curve and line are set by eye.

You can give a final smoothing by using the outside edge of the gouge. Hold it at an angle like a skew and run it lightly over the surface of the piece.

Use the small gouge, first, to make a half-cove on the inside of each ring.

Use a gouge to trim down the ends of the stretcher.

Then use it to make a half-bead on the outside of each ring.

For now leave the ends with a constant diameter. It will be tapered after we make our final length measurements.

The center stretcher so far. Before tapering the ends, we will turn the side stretchers.

Load the billet into the lathe and round it roughly. Set the diameter at 1¾" using the caliber and the parting tool.

Shape from the center to each end. The ends should come down to about ¾" for now.

With the large gouge establish the diameter for the whole length of the stretcher.

When you get to this point it is time to set the stretcher aside for a couple of days. The wood, being green, will change some, so just before it is time to assemble the chair I will go back and do the final turning. The same is true for the legs.

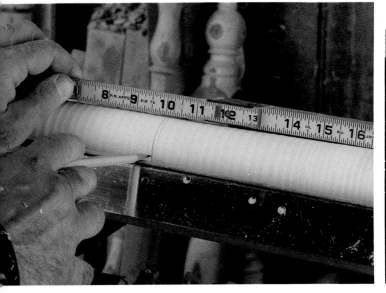

Measure and mark the center.

The legs and stretchers turned.

# Turning the Posts

The billet for the post is 14″ long, for a finished size of 13″. Round it down to a diameter of 1⅝″.

With the parting tool, define the segments.

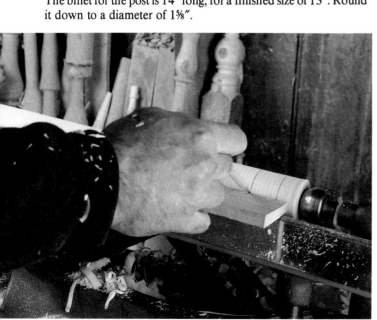

Mark the rings in the same way you did with the legs.

The taper of the tenon that goes into the arm begins at 5/8″ and goes to 7/16″.

The tenon that goes into the seat ends at ⅝".

Shape the lower vase. . .

The top of the seat tenon is 1".

trim the arm tenon end and shape the upper vase.

The end of the arm tenon is 7/16". Everything else is done by eye, referring to the measured drawings.

Shape the arm tenon

Shape the seat tenon.

Use the ladyfinger gouge to create a cove under the wafer and above the bead.

Use the skew to shape a bead.

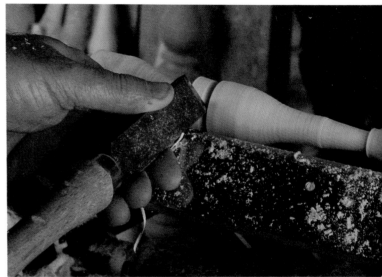

Create a wafer at the base of the top vase using the skew.

At the bottom of the vase form a wafer by incising a cut with the skew and cutting back under it.

Below that create a cove with a ½″ gouge.

Use a large gouge to shape the vases, rounding down the bottoms.

Use the skew to smooth the post.

Add glue lines to the tenons.

Use fine sandpaper to smooth the piece further.

Polish it off with wood shavings.

# Splitting for the Spindles, Comb, and Arm

Split a wedge from a 31″ log of red oak. Red oak splits much more easily than either white or black oak. It has the porous quality you need for the comb, but you could also use walnut, hickory, or other porous type woods. Use the froe to remove any faulty sections of the wood, like this deflection in the grain.

Drive the froe all the way in. . .

then use it as a lever to pry the wood apart. I find that if I angle the froe a little bit, I get more leverage.

A wedge works nicely to remove the some of the sap wood.

We want this center section for the comb. The sap wood (beneath the bark) is more likely to have fungi and other problems, while the heart wood has more inconsistencies in the grain.

Most of the work is done with the froe.

Sometimes the job is made easier if the billet is narrowed. The comb will be 3″ so we can safely trim the billet down to 5″ using the froe.

The split billet for the comb. The dimensions of the billet are both longer and wider than the finished comb will be. This gives plenty of space to compensate for planing.

Now use the froe to thin the billet.

For the bow and the spindles you need a piece roughly 48″ long.

Mark it for splitting at about 1½″, which will allow for minor adjustments through the splitting. The sap wood here is to be split off and discarded.

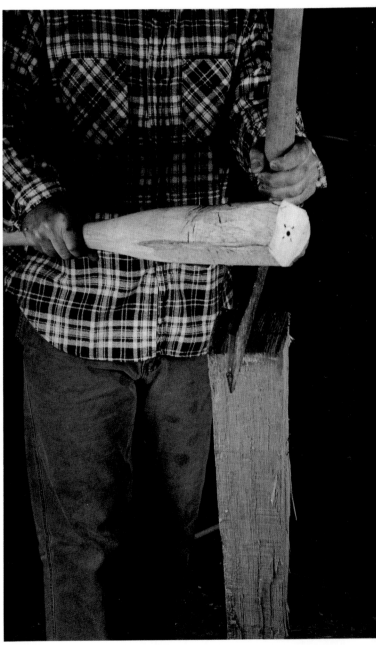

Begin your splitting at the line that is closest to halfway through the billet. Always try to divide the billet in halves.

36

Use the froe to pry the halves apart.

and one more time. This gives you billets that are approximately 1″ square to be used for the arm and spindles.

Now split one of the halves again. . .

# Seeing Defects

Sometimes you can see an interior defect in the grain by examining the bark, and sometimes you can't. This smaller diameter log of red oak looks great from the outside. . .

but when it is split the problems show up. This is not usable, except perhaps for the short spindles.

The comb back Windsor has seven long spindles (28″) and four short spindles (12″). Again you use oak, ash, or hickory. Use wedges to section the log.

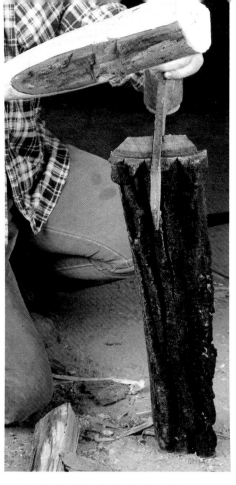

Split the billet in half with a froe.

Then split the outside section in half.

Continue the process until you get billets about an inch square.

The spindle billets ready for shaping.

The broad axe works well for these thinner splits.

# Shaping the Comb

A wood cleat fastened to the bench at one end and the vise at the other work together to hold the piece in place for planing. Two cleats, angled away from each other, also work nicely to hold a piece. You simply slide piece into the "V" until both ends are snugly held by the cleats.

Use a jack plane to plane the surface of the comb piece. The blade of the jack plane has a slight radius for taking off the bulk of the wood. The joiner plane is longer and has a straight blade. It makes the surface flat. The smoother plane is smaller than either, and takes off any rough spots that are left. The piece is now 30″ x 4″ x ⅞″, but will finish out at 28″ x 3¼″. The thickness will be reduced somewhat as we plane the board, but we don't want it too much thinner. Smooth both sides.

Place the piece on edge in the vise and use a joiner or jack plane to join the edge.

Lay the pattern on the piece so the flat side is along the planed edge of the board. Mark first one end. . .

then the other.

Cut the pattern of the comb. If you are a purist you will want to use a turning bow saw, like this. If not, a bandsaw works just fine.

Pick the best side as the face, then mark the center of the top.

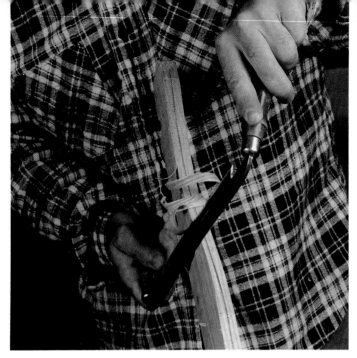

On the central portion of the comb taper the top one third of the front and back surfaces to the center line. Start at the center and work out. Cut with the grain, changing directions as the grain changes.

At the ears, the front stays relatively flat, and back is rounded to it.

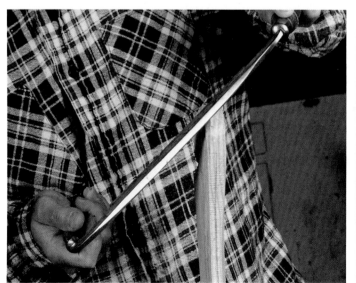

Round the back of the ears using the draw knife.

The ear section is also thinner than the rest of the comb, and tapers toward the end.

Here I cut with the grain and create curls. . .

which I then trim by coming back from the center of the comb.

To cut the curve under the ear, turn the drawknife upside down so the bevel is against the wood. An alternative for cleaning up this area under the ear is to use a file. For those who are uncomfortable or unfamiliar with the drawknife, this might be an easier way.

I need to go back with my joiner plane and take a little more off the face and back surfaces. This brings the comb down to a ¾″ thickness. It is important to get it as thin as you want before the bending to guard against splintering. The whole integrity of the chair relies on each piece contributing to the overall design. If the comb were heavier it would appear bulky and out of place. This is one of the reasons that the Windsor chair has developed to this point. You may not see this difference when the parts are separate. You may think it would work to change part of the design. Believe me when I say that when the chair is all together you will notice the difference immediately.

Use a spokeshave to round over the back of the ear. If you were to carve the ear, which is sometimes done, you would do the carving before you bend the comb.

Go over the whole piece with the spokeshave. Your object is to thin the upper edge while leaving the bottom thicker and strong. At the same time, and more importantly, you are giving it the nice, delicate look that is the hallmark of a fine Windsor chair.

43

Draw in the pattern to be carved into the face of the ears. Leave ⅛″ to 3/16″ lip around the outside of the ear. The pattern may vary somewhat from the one in the drawings, depending on the exact size of the comb's ear.

Go back over the stop cut with the knife, deepening the cut and trimming the gouge shavings.

Make a stop cut around the edge of the piece using a knife or a chisel. Begin with a light cut, and go back over it to deepen it. The final depth of the carving will be ⅛″.

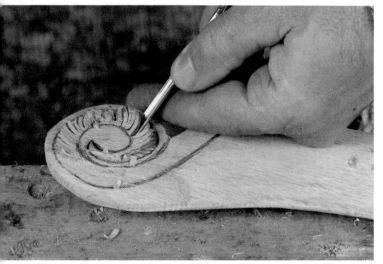

With a small gouge, carve back to the stop cut. I will smooth the ridges left by the gouge, but some may wish for them to remain and form a spiraling detail in the carving. The gouge should go deeper as it moves toward the stop cut.

With a low, flat sweeping gouge, I go back over the marks created by the smaller gouge and smooth them out.

Continue refining with chisels, gouges, and knives until the spiral reaches the shape you desire. The rough carving is done, and will be refined after bending.

Mark the center of the comb.

# Preparing the Arm

With the arm piece in the vise, use the draw knife to shape it to roughly 1″ x 1″.

With the piece on the bench, continue the shaping process using the jack. . .

and joiner planes. Continue until the four sides are square to one another with the dimensions of ⅝″ thick x ⅞″ wide x 45″ long. I leave the ends a little wider to accommodate the scroll part of the arms. The arms have glued-up pieces of poplar at the ends to accommodate the scroll. This will be discussed later.

Measure and mark the center.

I mark the inside of the arm "IN" with an arrow on the top surface which will point up when it is put in the shaping form.

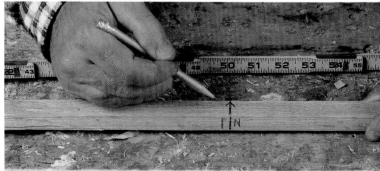

# Shaving the Spindles

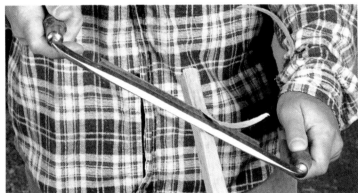

The spindles for the comb back Windsor need to be 27″ long. This allows for a 1¼″ tenon in the seat and a ¾″ tenon in the comb, with a 25″ exposure. Begin by rounding the bottom six inches of the spindle. I begin on the edges, holding the draw knife at a skewed angle to help it slice more easily. At the end the spindle will be ⅝″ in diameter, so we try to get close to that at this stage for the last two inches.

The bottom 1¼″ is the tenon size of ⅝″.

From there to the six inch mark is the heaviest portion of the spindle, tapering out to ¾″.

From the 6″ mark to the 10″ mark it tapers gradually to ⅜″.

The ⅜″ dimension continues over the top ten inches of the spindle.

To use you simply slide it over the end. Shave away excess wood until the gauge reaches the appropriate mark.

The gauge for measuring these dimensions is a scrap piece of wood, with holes for the ⅜″ dimension and the ⅝″ (when using green wood for the spindles you want to ream these holes out so they are just slightly larger than the stated dimensions. This allows for shrinkage as the wood dries). The ¾″ dimension is done by eye. The extra holes in this gauge are for other chairs.

You trim the top of the spindle in the same way as the bottom. You are trying to take long continuous slices, which will help you achieve an even dimension. Continue with the draw knife until you are almost to the final dimension. This reduces the amount of work you will need to do with the much finer spokeshave. Don't work on one side too long or you will go seriously out of round. Turn the piece often.

After the bottom tenon and the top is done I work on the middle, "swollen" section, bringing it into proportion to the bottom and top. You use smaller strokes in this area.

I use a smaller spokeshave. It is made of wood, and does not have the brass plate that some do. The plate is to protect it from wear, but I find that the wear helps the spokeshave follow the contour of the spindle.

When you get close to the final dimension, shift to the spokeshave for a finer finish.

Use the gauge to check the diameter.

49

Continue to work on the top. I have turned the drawknife over to get a little more control. As the top gets thinner, I like to work closer to the vise. This avoids bouncing and makes the work more efficient.

Finish up with the spoke shave.

Work your way from the tip to the bottom, checking with the gauge as you go.

The gauge has another use. With the gauge on the end of the work, it presses against your stomach and helps stabilize the piece as you work your way down the spindle. It's called Yankee ingenuity!

The spoke shave is roughly 10″ long, so it acts as a quick measure of where I want the ⅜″ dimension to end.

# Bending

The jig for bending the arm. The half round is 17½″ x 11″ x 2″. A cleat behind it allows for the wedge, and two holes near the front corners are for the pegs that hold the arm in place while it dries.

The steamer consists of a capped PVC tube 4″—6″ in diameter, suspended from the ceiling. I found an old copper still in a flea market in which I heat the water. The heat source is a camping stove. From the still a radiator hose feeds the steam into the steaming tube. The tube hangs at an angle to allow condensing water to drip out. Remember to put a pan under the lower end to catch the water.

Green wood needs 25-30 minutes to steam; dry wood needs 45 minutes to an hour. I pull out the wood with tongs because it is quite hot.

The wood goes immediately to the jig. This must be quick or the wood will cool and be unbendable. You have approximately one minute before it starts to cool!

Lock the piece in with the wedge.

Repeat the process on the other side. This is where problems may occur because the wood may cool. Basically you have 30 seconds to complete the whole bending, so you must be both careful and quick.

With a steady motion bend one end around the jig. Listen for cracks. If you hear them you may need to steam it more or bend it more slowly.

The bent arm on the jig.

When the bending is complete, hold it in place with the peg and move quickly to the other side.

The jig for the comb is in two piece, and uses three bar clamps to create the bending.

When the comb has been steamed for 45 minutes to an hour, lay it between the two forms, aligning the centers as closely as possible.

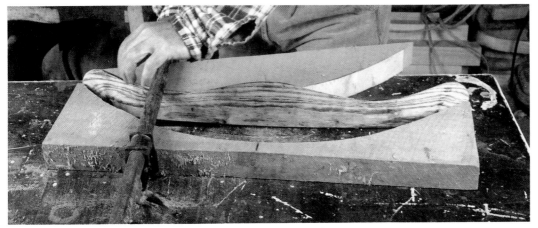

Set a clamp on one side.

Squeeze it as closely as possible.

Add a clamp to the other side, squeezing it as much as it will go.

Alternately tighten the two clamps. When the outside clamps are threaded out, place the center clamp and tighten it down.

You can then reset the outside clamps one at a time. Tighten the center clamp as you go.

The bent comb. The center mark may shift, but the curve will still be good.

# An Alternative: Joining Planks for the Seat

Check the joint for tightness. There should be no movement or gaps along the joint line.

While I manage to buy trees that produce single plank seats, that is not always possible. It is easy to join two narrower pieces into a lovely seat. These pine boards are roughly 2″ thick x 10 wide x 22″ long. They have air dried for about a year.

Continue the process until the joint is as near perfect as you can get it. The old-time cabinet makers were famous for their invisible joints. With perseverance you should be able to do the same.

To get a smooth glue surface, use a joiner plane with a smooth stroke using even pressure throughout. If you fail to do this, you may get a depression that will hinder the joining of the two planks.

While there are many new glues, I prefer to use the yellow carpenters glue. Three or four pipe clamps provide the pressure you need for a strong joint. Adjust the clamps before applying the glue. Alternate both the direction of the clamps (left -right) and position (top -bottom).

Apply a thin coat of glue to size the surface of the wood. Let it dry for about three minutes until it becomes tacky. This allows the wood to absorb the glue.

Set the clamps.

Apply a second coat of glue, and let it set up for about 1 minute. Yellow glue should be used within 3 minutes for maximum bonding strength, so this gives you two minutes to finish.

Move from clamp to clamp, tightening a little more each time. You don't want to tighten too extremely.

You can rub the joints together to help the bonding.

Check the joint to make sure it does not move. When you achieve an adequate pressure set it aside to dry for at 24 hours.

# Sculpting the Seat

Use the jack plane and the joiner plane to smooth the flat surfaces of the seat plank. With a wide piece like this it is likely that it has acquired a slight bow as it dried. Go at a slight diagonal as you plane across the grain.

In the planing we found this knot. We'll put this on the underside of the chair. This is one of the reasons for planing at this point.

When you have achieved a flat surface, plane with the grain to smooth out the marks you have created.

Turn the board over and repeat the process.

Lay the pattern on the board and mark the center lines. . .

Continue the center and side lines onto the seat itself.

and side lines.

Then draw the outline of the pattern.

Cut the seat using a turning bow saw. Again, non-purists can use a bandsaw.

Draw a 2″ line around the back of the seat using a pencil and a rule as a guide. Start at one of the side lines and go to the other.

The side lines define the end of the spindle area.

The center line in the back is the point of the center spindle.

Freehand, draw a line from the corner of the side line to the center of the front edge in an approximate radius. It's O. K. to use your best judgement—you have permission not to be perfect!

The seat area is defined. The cross section in the middle is to help you visualize the contour of the seat. It is deepest toward the back, and tapers gradually back up as it moves to the front. At its lowest point the hollow is about ¾″.

The hollow rises to this line, and then tapers down again toward the front edge.

Continue rounding toward the top. Notice that I only go halfway, working out from the center. This is because the grain changes, so I need to work in different directions.

These are the basic tools for rounding the back edge of the seat: a block plane, two sizes of spoke shave, and the draw knife.

Round the bottom edge of the chamfer.

Begin with a 45 degree chamfer on the bottom back edge, using the drawknife.

Switch to the larger spokeshave to smooth the marks. The spoke-shave is actually a push tool, but when it is convenient, I sometimes pull it like this. Repeat the process on the other side of the bottom.

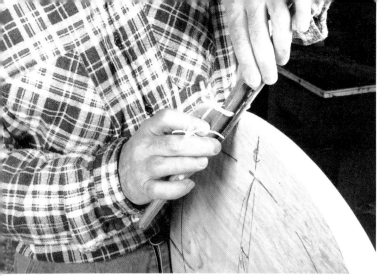

Now I use the spokeshave to put a slight chamfer on the top edge of the back.

The chamfer will go all the way to ⅛″ from the top edge of the front. Stop with the drawknife about ¼″ from the top edge, and finish the work with a plane.

Continue the process on the sides. The shaving here is harder because we are going across end grain. Be patient!

Go over the chamfer with a block or smoothing plane.

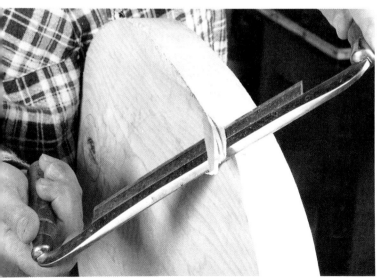

On the front we will use a different technique. On the underside of the front make a deep 45 degree chamfer with the drawknife.

Returning to the drawknife, blend the chamfer of the sides with that of the front.

61

Take out the marks with the spoke shave.

The shaped bottom.

The basic tools for doing the top of the seat. We work from the most aggressive to the finer tools. Start with the gutter adz, move to the scorp, the round-bottomed radius plane, and finally to a round bottom metal spokeshave. Both of the latter tools were adapted.

Place your feet at the end of the board to hold it in place (steel toed shoes are strongly recommended), and use the gutter adz to remove the area of the seat. Use nice, smooth strokes.

Good follow-through is important here. Because of the radius line of a gutter adz, make the swing of the cut on a similar line and do not allow the leading cutting edge to dig in.

As you work from the side toward the center the grain changes, so you have to change direction as you work.

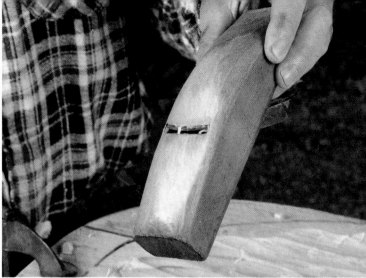

If you don't have a scorp you can customize a block plane, rounding the foot and the blade to match the radius of your seat. In fact, the whole job could be done with this customized plane.

The gutter adz removes a lot of wood in a hurry.

The plane also helps smooth the lines left by the scorp.

Use the scorp to smooth the lines left by the adz.

The flatter the curve of the blade, the smoother the work. Each step of sculpting the seat has a smoother effect. Use the curved plane to take down the front edge of the seat, on either side of the center, which remains at full thickness. .

The final step is done with a metal spokeshave. I customized it from a straight metal one by filing the sole into a curve to a slight radius. Then I cut the arms back so they wouldn't get in the way. A wooden travisher with a radius sole was traditionally used for making Windsor seats, but they are extremely rare on the second hand tool market today. Travisher remakes are available, but are expensive. An inexpensive metal spokeshave takes less than an hour to reshape and you can achieve excellent finishing results with a little practice.

Then go with the grain to smooth things further. It will take some practice to learn this technique.

With the spokeshave, first go across the grain at a slight diagonal to even things out.

The seat is shaped, and no sandpaper was necessary, though you can use it to round over any sharp edges or loose fibers.

# Preparing the Seat
# for Legs and Spindles

Place your pattern over the top side of shaped seat. Align it with the marks. Through the holes in the pattern, mark the points for the legs and the spindles and posts.

The post holes are placed slightly in from center. This allows for the angle of the post.

Make sure the spindle marks are half way between the concave portion of the seat and the back edge.

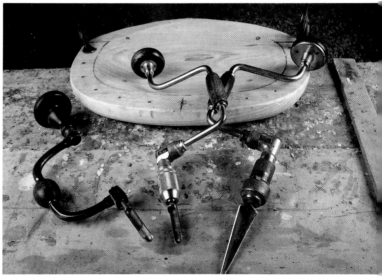

To drill holes for the legs, posts, and spindles, I use a brace and bit. I keep three braces, one for each bit. For the spindles I use a 9/16″ spoon bit. For the legs and posts I use a ⅝″ spoon bit for the pilot hole. I then use a tapered reamer, between 8 and 10 degrees.

Clamp the seat to the bench with the saddle side up. Begin with the back legs. They are splayed about 110 degrees back and 100 degrees to the side. To set the angle use two bevel squares set to the proper angles with a protractor. The angle here is not fixed in granite. Don't be upset if the leg angle is not exactly 110 degrees. Practice on a scrap piece and develop your adjustments by eye without the use of any jigs. You will be surprised by the amount of confidence you will gain by allowing yourself the freedom to develop this way.

Align the bevel squares on the bench with the line of the leg. Start drilling perpendicular to the surface, and gradually move the brace to align with the angles of the bevel squares.

Go about half way with the spoon bit, stopping occasionally to check the angle. Remember, these angles are somewhat intuitive. Use your eye and your sense of beauty!

Repeat the process on the other rear leg.

The same process is used for the front, with the opposite angles. The front to back angle is 100 degrees and the side-to-side angle is between 105 and 110 degrees. Start the bit at perpendicular and move it out to the proper angle.

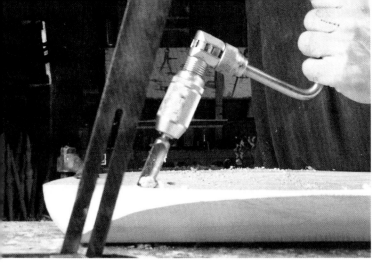

The angles should match in one direction. . . .

Check the legs for fit. With one leg in place bore the other. The brace itself acts as a rough guide to the angle.

and the other.

With the seat in the vise, use the tapered bit to make the leg hole. Drill from the bottom, following the line created by the spoon bit. Two things to be careful of! First, the seat in the vise is subject to breaking if too much pressure is applied, so be gentle. Second, don't drill all the way with the tapered bit. The widest point of the taper is approximately 1″ in diameter. Leave room for any final adjustment after the legs are in place. We will expand on this concept shortly.

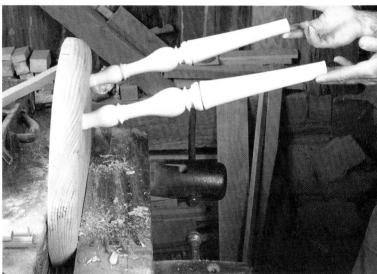

Place the second leg in the hole and check for the proper depth and alignment.

Lay a straight edge across the back and use the bevel square to check your angles.

Do the same on both back legs.

The right front leg is coming out at too great an angle.

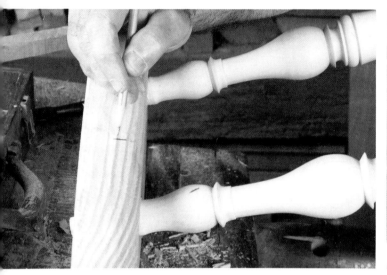

Mark each socket and leg pair 1, 2, 3, or 4 as you complete it. Each leg is mated with a particular socket, and if you switch them around they may not fit as well during assembly.

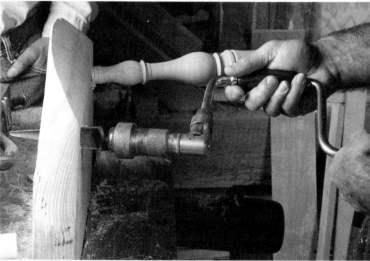

To adjust for this I return to the tapered bit, and manipulate it so that it only cuts on the inside of the hole. In other words, when the cutting edge is on the inside I apply pressure, and when it is on the outside I lessen the pressure.

Repeat the process in the front. As you bore the hole, hold the brace as steadily as you can to assure an even socket.

On a flat surface, put the legs in place.

Tap them in. Be sure not to over bang, because the tapers of the legs can act as a wedge and split your seat.

Measure between the front and back legs from scribe mark to scribe mark. Here we have a difference in the measurements of almost a half inch.

Line up the front legs on the edge of your bench.

The left rear leg is the problem, so I mark the direction it needs to move on the bottom of the seat.

Go back with the tapered bit. Two or three turns may make enough difference, so measure early and often.

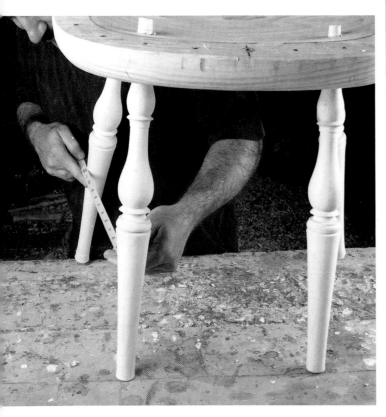

Two turns made the angle correct.

Line up the front legs with the edge of the table again. When looking at it from the front, the chair should look balanced. The secret of chair making is the look of the chair, not drawings or jigs. In this case the chair looks straight and the angles of the legs are pleasing. It shouldn't turn to the right or left. If it does, it means either one of the front legs is not on the same angle and needs adjustment in or out. This is the reason the legs were not completely set at first. Now, with a little more taper you can make final adjustments.

# Measuring for
# the Stretchers

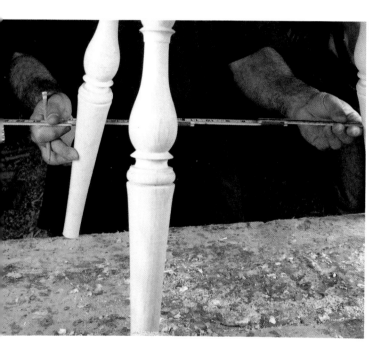

For the middle stretcher measure between the **inside** of one front leg to the **outside** of the other at the scribe mark. It measures 18⅜″.

Do the same measurement between the back legs. This measures 11⅜″.

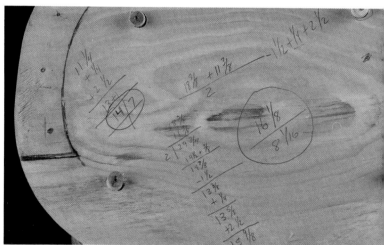

I do the calculation for the stretchers on the seat. This keeps it handy for reference. To find the length of the medial stretcher, add the front measurement (18⅜″) and the back measurement (11⅜″). The sum is 29¾″. Divide this sum by two (14⅞″).

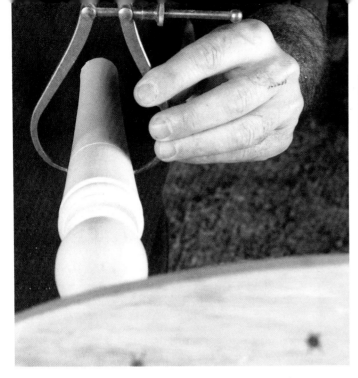

Subtract the thickness of the leg at scribe (1½″). This brings you to 13⅜″.

Measure between the scribe marks (inside to inside) to determine the length of the stretcher. Both measure 11¼″.

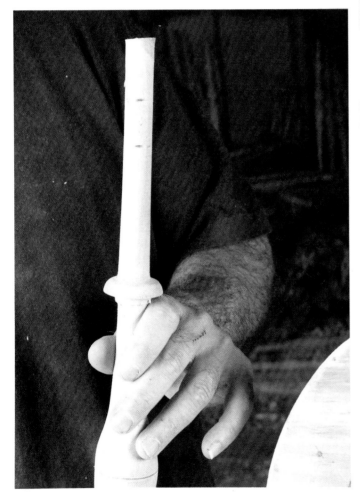

Add ¼″ to create tension in the leg (equals 13⅝″). Finally add 2½″, which is the total of the two tenons of the stretcher. This gives you a total length of 16⅛″, or 8 1/16″ from the center point to either end.

The side stretchers are 11¼″, plus ¼″ for tension, plus 2½″ for the two tenons for a total length of 14″. This equals 7″ from the center to either end.

# Final Turnings for the Stretchers

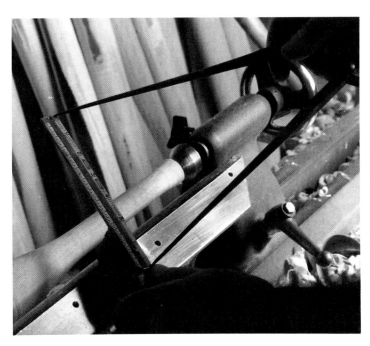

Return the piece turned for the side stretcher to the lathe. Set the divider at 7".

Set a second divider at 1¼" and mark the length of the tenon at each end from the 7" mark toward the center.

Mark the points seven inches to either side of the center.

Set a caliper to ⅝", which will be the thickness of the tenon.

Use a parting tool and the caliper to set the diameter of the tenon.

A skew will smooth the finish.

With the gouge, turn the tenons to size.

Use the parting tool to deepen the cut at the end of the tenon for separation later.

Shape the center portion of the stretcher to taper down to the tenon. The center should remain thick to receive the medial tenon.

Sand the stretcher. . .

and rub it down with wood chips.

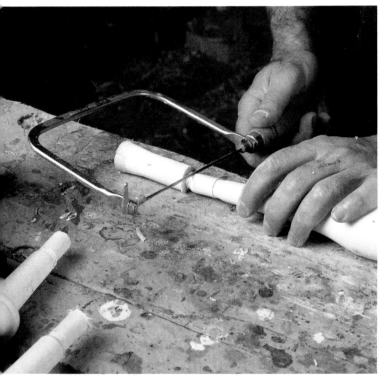

Use a coping saw to remove the ends.

The medial stretcher is prepared in the same way. With the piece in the lathe, begin by marking 8 1/16″ from the center with a divider. The medial stretcher contains an element called a ring. The ring consists of a half cove and bead located midway between the center scribe line and tenon.

# Assembling the Undercarriage

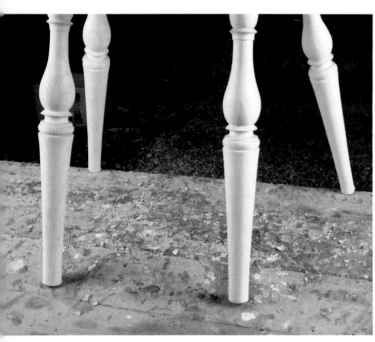

Returning to the undercarriage, line the front legs up with the edge of the bench.

Set the body of the bevel square along the front edge of the table and the blade along the straight edge. This is the angle drilled into the side stretcher to receive the medial stretcher.

Lay a straightedge along the outside of the legs, from front to back.

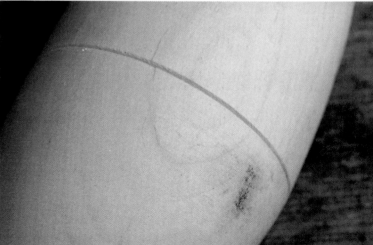

The hole needs to be drilled into the face grain of the side stretcher. The shrinkage is greater this way so it closes around the joint more tightly. The grain on the face has a circular pattern.

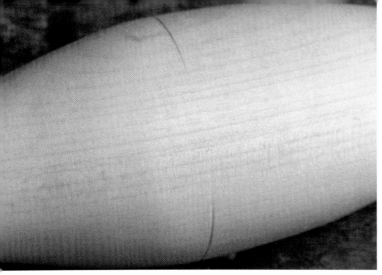

rather than the straight pattern on the side.

Go 1¼″ inch deep plus some for the depth of the tenon. I usually mark the depth on the spoon bit with a black marker or tape.

Drill into the center line with a 9/16″ inch spoon bit. Start perpendicular to the piece. . .

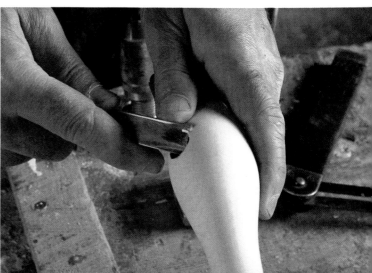

Use a chisel to bevel or clean the edge of the hole. The spoon bit bites into the end grain and leaves strands of wood to be cleaned.

then tilt the brace to match the angle of the bevel square.

Round the ends of the tenons with a chisel. This will make it match the shape left by the spoon bit.

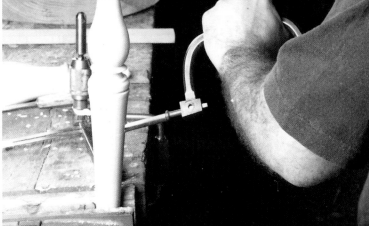

Shave the sides of the tenon with the chisel until you get a tight fit. You should be able to push it about half way into the hole by hand, and tap it the rest of the way. The flat spots created by the chisel help wedge the tenon in place.

and gradually move to the angle of the stretcher.

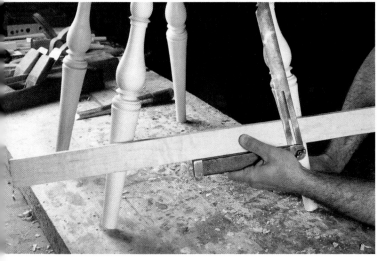

To determine the angle of the mortise hole in the front legs, hold a straight edge on the scribe marks on the front and back leg. Set your bevel square to the angle formed by the straight edge and the center of front leg.

About halfway into the hole check the angle with the bevel and make adjustments.

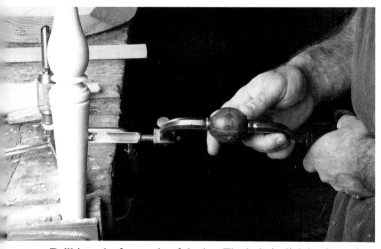

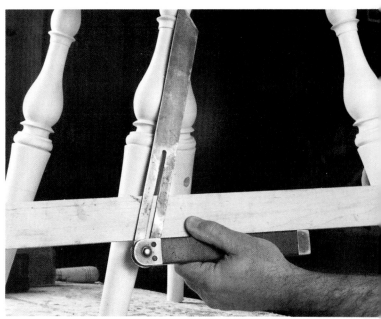

Drill into the face grain of the leg. The hole is slightly above the scribe line on the front legs and slightly below it on the back. This will make the stretcher plane parallel to the plane of the seat. Start straight in. . .

Repeat the process with the back legs.

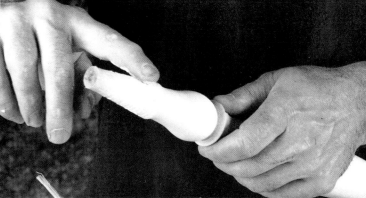

Now you are ready to assemble the undercarriage. I use white glue for the undercarriage. It takes longer to set, which gives me more time for adjustments. Set the legs beside the seat, near their final positions.

Apply glue to the tenons of the legs. Work it into the surface by rubbing it with a finger. White glue is not carcinogenic or toxic, so don't worry.

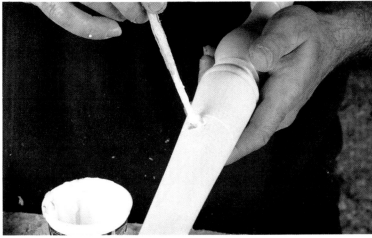

Apply glue to all the holes and to the tenons of the stretchers.

Place a second dab of glue in the mortises of the legs.

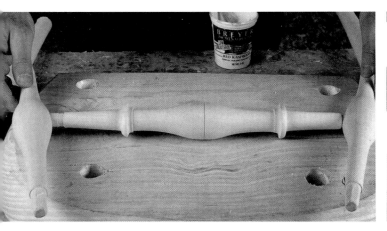
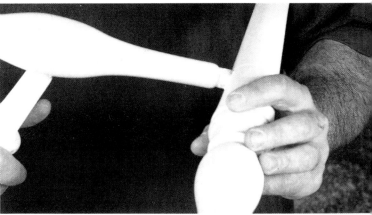

Align the stretcher assembly by laying it on a flat surface.

Tap the stretcher in place.

Insert the stretcher assembly into one of the front legs.

Put the leg lightly in place in the seat and align the stretcher.

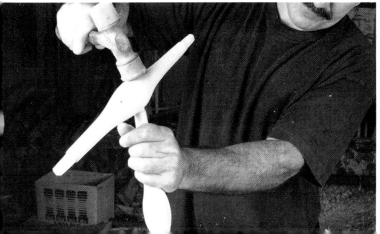
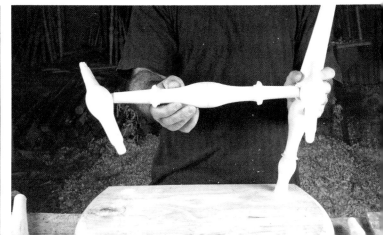

Remove the leg and tap the stretcher in place. Use a plastic or wooden mallet.

Add the other three legs, one at a time.

Take the undercarriage assembly out of the seat and tap the joints into place.

Realign the legs in the seat.

Working your way around the legs, tap them home. The legs have a delicate balance. Keep moving from leg to leg. Turn the seat 180 degrees or perpendicular to the front edge of the table to insure against splitting along the grain.

Take a step or two back and make sure your alignment is correct.

Cut off protruding ends of the tenons, leaving about ⅛″.

Use a drawknife to make a wedge from a piece of scrap. It should be a little wider than the end of the tenon. This helps it set into the seat as well as the tenon, so it resists the twisting motion when someone sits in the seat. Taper the sides slightly at the ends to help the wedges drive in more easily.

Apply glue to the ends of the wedge and rub it in.

With a chisel cut into the tenon and seat. Be certain to go **across the grain**, or you will surely split the seat.

Drive the wedge into the cut. Do not drive too far. Listen for a sound change from the initial sharp taps to the duller thud sound to help determine when to stop. If you go too far the tenon could act as a wedge and split the seat.

Cut off the wedges.

81

Remove any remaining end of the tenon with a chisel, being sure to always cut toward the middle. Work your away around until it is free.

To trim the legs even to the floor, measure on each side of the seat where the arm posts are marked. This area is a flat horizontal section, making it easy to measure. They should be equal distance from the floor. If one side is higher it needs to be reduced by trimming the leg. In this case each side is 20¼".

The front of the seat should be 18" from the floor to the highest point. Our measure is 20¼", so it needs to come down 2¼".

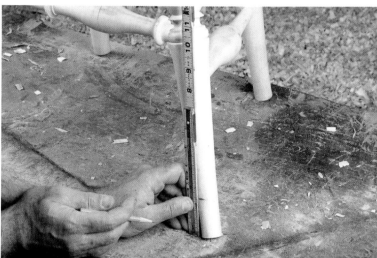

I'll mark each of the front legs at 2¼" from the floor.

Cut the front legs parallel with the floor or the surface you are working on.

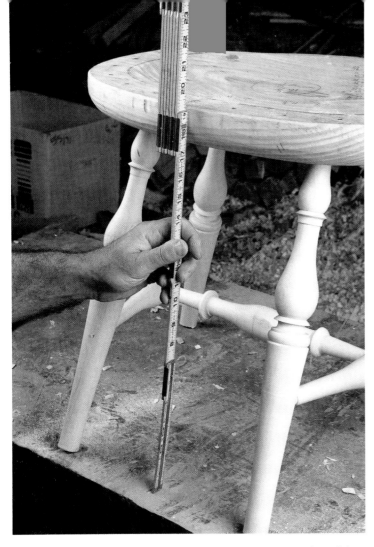

When that is done, stand the chair on your bench with the three trimmed legs on the bench and one leg hanging over the edge. Be sure the seat is as flat as you want it. Then simply cut off the fourth leg even with the surface of the bench.

The measurement at the back should be ½″ less than that of the front or 17½″. Measure the center. We need to take off 1¾″ to get where we want to be.

Mark one of the back legs and cut the bottom parallel to the floor.

The finished seat and undercarriage.

# Assembling the Upper Chair

To prepare the arm for the addition of a piece to be scrolled, place the joiner plane in a vise with the blade up.

Do the same with the piece you will be using for the scroll. I use poplar because its grain structure makes it less likely to split than oak.

Run the outside surface of the arm over the plane to get a good glue joint.

This gives you a good flat surface.

Situate the addition on the arm and mark for alignment. Because I may be gluing more than one arm at a time, marking the pieces adds a little insurance.

Apply a thin coat of glue to each of the four surfaces. This will size the joint. Depending on shop temperatures, allow this to set for approximately 3 minutes. In the past chairmakers inserted pins through the scroll piece into the arm, to secure the hide glue joint. Because this is a reproduction piece and because modern glue works better, yellow glue is recommended for a more lasting bond.

When the first coat of glue has dried, apply a second, more generous coat to all four surfaces. Let it set for a minute or so.

Rub the surface together before aligning them.

Apply the first clamp lightly. The piece will move if you tighten it too much too soon.

Apply the second clamp and tighten it. Remember, it is important not to overtighten. If you use too much pressure, the glue may squeeze out and starve the joint. The joint will fail after a short period of time.

Go from one to the other until you have a good tight bond. Do not over tighten or you will squeeze out the glue you need.

I use a block plane, principally for convenience. It is small enough not to be interfered with by the vise.

Ready to be set aside overnight.

Another way to plane the arm would be to clamp it to the table. A jack or joiner plane can be used as well. Plane all four surfaces.

The next day, remove clamps and mount the piece in the vise. The additional piece is thicker than the arm, so we need to plane it to the thickness of the arm.

Lay the scroll pattern on the end of the arm and trace it.

The drawn pattern.

round the edge with a spokeshave.

Cut the pattern with the coping saw.

If you feel comfortable using them, various wood files. . .

Use a spokeshave to clean the saw marks and. . .

and rattail rasps help smooth the places the spokeshave can't reach.

A drawknife can also come in handy. Use whatever tool you are comfortable with to get the job done. My preference is the draw knife, but it does take some practice to learn to use it.

Smooth the work with a cabinet scraper. The cabinet scraper works well on the flat surfaces of the arm, outside. . .

Continue the smoothing onto the arm, cleaning the outside of the arm with the spokeshave.

as well as the inside.

As more of the arm is exposed, stabilize and support it with your body.

Use the cabinet scraper to smooth the spindles. The goal is not to make them round, but simply to clean up the rough spots.

Make four short (12″) spindles for the front of the arms. The base is ⅝″ in diameter and the top is 7/16″. The 7/16″ measurement will go down the spindle a few inches.

Use the scraper to clean up the comb.

Go over the spindles with sandpaper. This is not a hard sanding, but a quick, light once over to remove any "hairs" left from scraping.

The carving on the ears of the comb can be cleaned with a chisel, using a scraping motion.

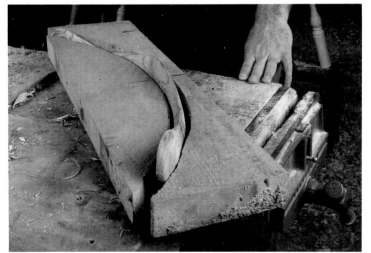

The comb, having sat for a few days, is ready to be removed from the jig. There will be some spring-back when it is taken out, but the jig was designed with enough curve to compensate for that.

Sand it to get the final smoothing.

Go over the whole comb with sandpaper.

After you get the hole started, slant the bit forward and out. This is pretty much by eye, but I move the brace about 2″ forward and 2″ out to the side.

The parts are ready for assembly.

Follow the hole with the tapered reamer. The biggest part of the tenon is 1″ in diameter, so go to a diameter a little less than that to leave room for adjustment.

Start a pilot hole for the arm posts at a perpendicular angle, using a ⅝″ spoon bit.

Test the arm post for the proper fit.

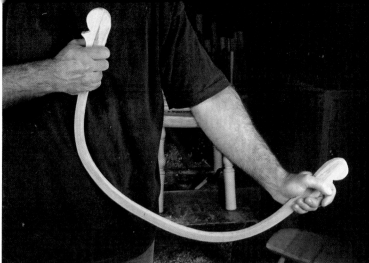

To check the angle run a straight edge across the seat and set your bevel square to the angle of one post.

If the curve of the arm is too tight, you can bend it out until it fits.

Move it to the other side. If the angles do not match, make adjustments using the tapered reamer.

Ideally the post should enter the arm at the thickest portion. . .

Line up the back of the arm so that its inside edge is about even with the outside back edge of the seat when you look straight down at it. Check to be sure everything is balanced.

but it does not have to be exact. In fact, this time it comes a little in front of the first mark I made. Mark the point where the arm post will come through, and the side of the arm at the angle of the arm post.

With the arm in a vise, use a 7/16″ spoon bit to drill through the top of the arm. Start the hole perpendicular and move to the proper angle. The hole should angle in and toward the back as it goes down.

Finish the hole with the reamer from the bottom. Ream it so the entry hole is roughly ⅝″ in diameter. Repeat on the other side.

To check your fit hold the arm in place and measure perpendicularly from the seat at the back of the post to the top of the arm. It should be between 8″ and 9″. Again, this measurement is relative to your table height. Most table heights are approximately 29″. With a seat height of 18″ and the arm another 8″ or 9″, there is a total height of 26″ or 27″, just enough to fit under an average table. So check your table height; you may need to adjust the chair a half inch or so.

Do the same on the other side. If they do not match, use the reamer to make adjustments to the hole.

With the arm in place, measure from the seat to the top of the middle of the arm. It should be about ½″ less than the measurement at the post. If it's not exact you should have room to move the arm up or down a little for this adjustment. If not, you may have to go back and readjust your angled holes in the arm so it does tilt back some.

Starting with the center hole use a spoon bit to make the holes in the seat for the spindles. The center hole should be straight up and down and slightly back. These spindle holes do not go all the way through, but go about 1¼″.

The other holes for the long spindles should be slightly back and fan at slight angles to the outside. If you feel uncomfortable making the holes with the brace, go half way and stand back to check your angle; make sure it's not over-exaggerated. Remember, the spoon bit is capable of changing directions as needed. Its versatility at obtaining angles is why the spoon bit was known as the "chairmaker's bit".

The back holes for the shorter spindles should go slightly outside and slightly toward the front. This change in the direction of the spindles sets up opposing forces that bring stability to the back of the chair.

The front holes of the shorter spindles should follow the outward line of the post and be slightly more forward slanting than the other short spindles.

After cleaning out the holes, create a bevel around their edges with a chisel.

Use a block plane to clean up the area of the seat where the spindles will go.

Redraw your 2″ line if necessary.

93

With a small gouge (approximately ⅛″), follow the line of the spindle area, creating a nice decorative touch to separate the spindle area from the scooped out portion of the seat.

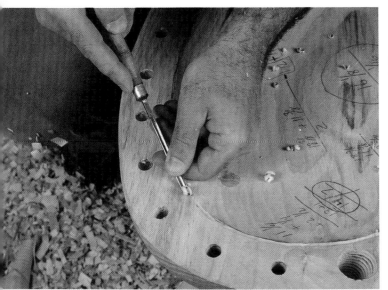

Be sure to go with the grain.

Use a round bottomed spokeshave to clean up any rough spots in the saddle area.

Do a final shaving of the spindles so they will fit in the holes. Shave definite flat spots so when driven into the sockets of the round holes they will form a tight fit.

Put the spindles in place, tapping them lightly. Do not drive them all the way into the sockets yet; be sure you can remove them.

Replace the arm posts and the arm. The back spindles are situated behind the arm and the shorter spindles are situated inside. With the chair on a level surface, align the middle spindle so it is plumb.

Using a divider take the distance between the spindles at the seat...

and transfer it to the arm, starting at the middle and working your way out.

The position of the short spindles is determined by dividing the segment of the arm between the post and the first long spindle into thirds.

Remove the spindles, but keep them in order so they can be replaced.

Use a ⅜" spoon bit to drill the holes for the long spindles. Support the arm with your knee and drill the holes for the long spindles, starting with the one in the center. If you aim for the corresponding hole in the seat, your angle should be good. Splitting is a danger at this point, so don't apply a lot of force. If you want to be particularly careful, apply a clamp to the arm. Non-purists may wish to use a power drill.

With the back spindles in place to support the arm, use a 7/16" spoon bit to make the holes for the short spindles.

Clean the holes with a chisel.

Remove the arm and clean the holes.

Test fit each spindle. They should go through the arm to a point where the top of the arm comes to 10" from the bottom of the spindle. Trim any spindles that are too thick. If a spindle is a little thin it will probably be alright, but if it is *too* loose it will affect the integrity of your chair.

Shape a glue stick from scrap.

Give the holes an initial coating of glue. This sizes the hole. A second coat is used to compensate for the lack of any glue on the spindle tenons.

Twist the post into place to increase the hold. The face grain should be on the inside and outside.

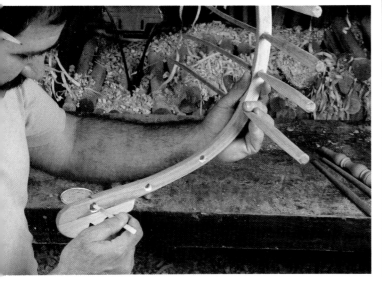

At the arm I glue only the short spindles and the post, not the long spindles.

Insert the short spindles through the arms.

Rub the tenon of the post with glue using your finger. This gets it into the wood. On this critical piece I use extra glue.

Join the back/arm assembly to the seat and posts.

Place the spindles in the holes and turn them until they arc properly aligned.

Tap the spindles in place. You will notice a dulling of the sound as they become seated.

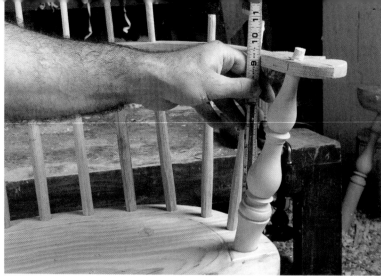

Measure at the arm. It should be 9″, so we need to tap it down.

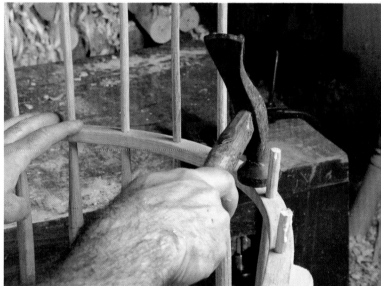

Tap a little at a time. . .

working your way around.

Move back for perspective and eyeball the arm to make sure it runs evenly, coming down to 8½" at the center back.

Glue the tips of the wedges...

Use the coping saw to cut the ends of the spindles and posts, leaving ⅛" protruding above the arm.

and drive them into the ends of the posts and spindles.

Cut slits in the posts with the chisel for the wedges. Cut across the grain.

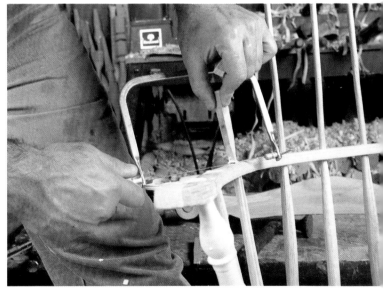

Saw off the wedges.

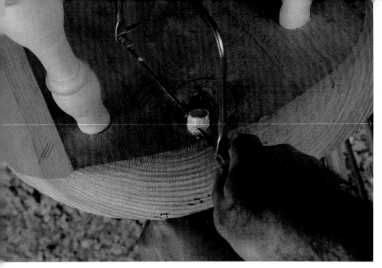

Cut the bottom of the post, leaving ⅛″. When you drive in the wedge this end will flare out, giving you a little extra hold.

Finish the top of the arm with the cabinet scraper.

Cut a slit and drive the wedge. Don't go too far or the seat may split. Trim the wedge.

Remark the center of the comb.

Use a drawknife to clean the top of the arm. A plane may also be used.

Drill the hole for the center spindle with a ⅜″ spoon bit. The depth should be approximately 1″.

Put the comb in place on the center spindle and clamp the outside spindles in place.

Make any final adjustments to the spacing. Then, holding the spindle in place, mark both sides of it. This gives the line for the hole. Repeat the process for each spindle.

Measure and adjust the comb until both sides are equal.

Take the comb to the vise and drill the holes, following the spacing and angles you have drawn.

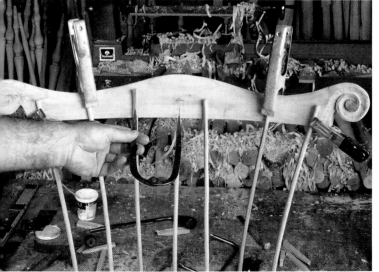

Clamp the next two spindles in place, using a divider to assure fairly equal spacing between each spindle. Continue to the inside pair.

Bevel the ends of the spindles.

Tap the comb into place for a test fitting.

When the fit is correct remark the position of the comb.

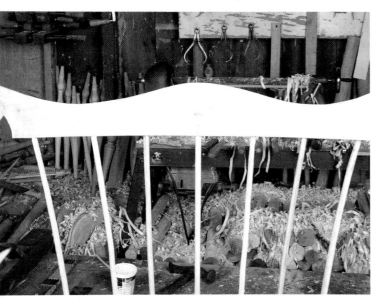

Check that the comb is parallel to the arm and level. Then mark where the bottom of the comb meets each spindle. This will not be the final placement of the comb. It simply give you a guideline for making adjustments.

Apply glue to the hole.

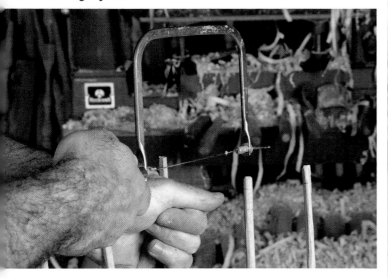

You may find that some of the spindles are a little too long. Trim them off with the coping saw.

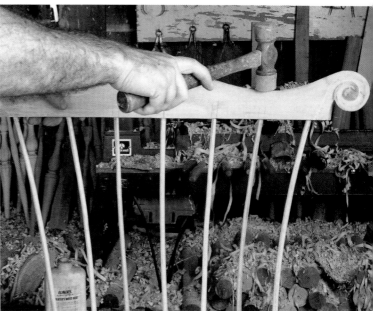

Reset the comb so it lines up with the marks.

102

When it is in place, drill holes for the pegs that will keep the spindles in place. The holes are 3/16″ or roughly half the diameter of the spindles.

and drive it into place. Holding a second hammer in the back will give you the support you need.

The pegs are drawn from dry scrap lumber.

Saw off the excess peg.

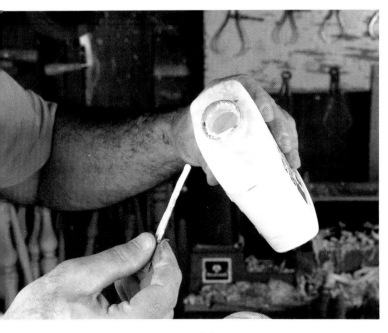

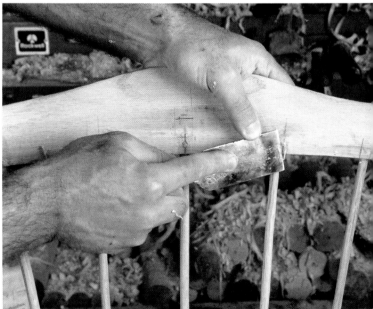

Put a dab of glue on the end of the peg. . .

Slice away the knobs of the pegs.

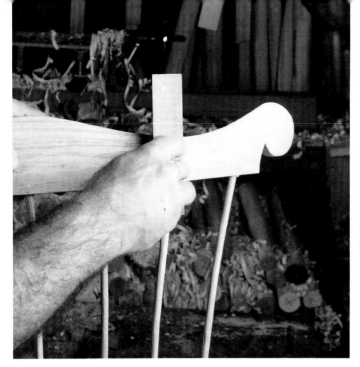

Use a scraper to get a nice smooth surface.

Rub excess glue away with a damp cloth.

Ready for sanding and scraping.

The primary and most authentic tool for smoothing is the cabinet scraper.

The pine of the seat makes it too soft to use the scraper effectively.

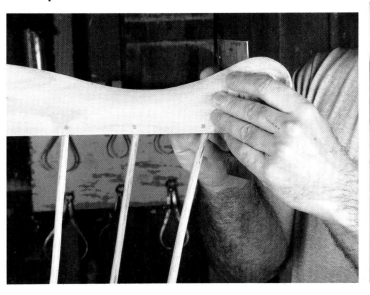

Go over the whole chair, removing sharp edges and generally smoothing surfaces.

Check the undercarriage for any glue drips and remove them with the chisel, followed by sandpaper.

I use sandpaper mostly on the areas of the chair that naturally would be worn by use. When Windsors were originally made there was no sandpaper. New finishes were rough, and were worn only by use. I use sandpaper primarily to recreate that soft smooth surface brought on by years of use, and not to remove the hand tool marks.

I also chamfer the ends of the legs. This helps keep them from chipping.

Ready for finishing.

# Finishing

I finish my chairs in milk paint mixed with water, which I go over with linseed oil after it dries. This is the traditional finish, in use for hundreds of years. I buy powder and mix the paint myself.

A quick test of the paint on the chair shows that it is too watery, so I simply add more powder.

Start with the undercarriage.

Traditionally the underside of the seat is left unpainted. The early chairmakers conserved materials whenever possible.

Continue on the upper portion of the chair.

Apply a second coat.

The first coat is finished. Let it dry for 10 or 15 minutes.

As the paint dries, it will take a lighter, milkier tone.

When it is totally dry, it is time for a rubbing with steel wool. Begin with 0 grade and rub all surfaces to remove the rough spots and grain raised by the milk paint.

If you come across a spot you missed, touch it up.

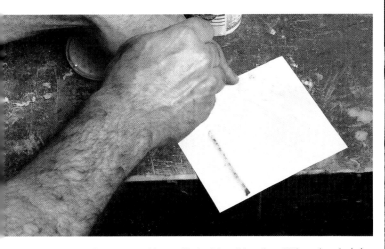

The label is paper and is applied with white glue. When the chair is oiled, the label will be oiled as well.

Branding irons are made by various companies for use in marking your chair.

Apply linseed oil with a brush or a dry, lint free cloth. Let it set 5 minutes and wipe away the excess.

The finished chair.

# Gallery

Different views of the comb back Windsor

The continuous arm Windsor.

A bird cage Windsor
in a brown finish.

A bird cage Windsor.

A sack back Windsor settee.

Lancaster style antique Windsor.

The bow back Windsor.

A sack back Windsor.